J327.124
POL

DISCARD.

D1261784

DISCARD

INSIDE THE WORLD'S MOST FAMOUS INTELLIGENCE AGENCIES

Inside France's DGSE
The General Directorate for External Security

Patti Polisar

The Rosen Publishing Group, Inc.
New York

This book is dedicated to the ones I love,
and to the spirit of Daniel Pearl.

Published in 2003 by The Rosen Publishing Group, Inc.
29 East 21st Street, New York, NY 10010

Copyright © 2003 by The Rosen Publishing Group, Inc.

First Edition

All rights reserved. No part of this book may be reproduced in any form without permission in writing from the publisher, except by a reviewer.

Library of Congress Cataloging-in-Publication Data
Polisar, Patti.
Inside France's DGSE: The General Directorate for External Security / by Patti Polisar.
   p. cm. — (Inside the world's most famous intelligence agencies)
Summary: An introduction to the history, functions, and current goals of France's intelligence agency, the DGSE or Direction générale de la sécurité extérieure.
Includes bibliographical references and index.
ISBN 0-8239-3814-X (lib. bdg.)
1. France. Direction générale de la sécurité extérieure—Juvenile literature. 2. Intelligence service—France—History—Juvenile literature. [1. Intelligence service—France—History.
2. Espionage—France—History. 3. Secret service—France.]
I. Title. II. Series.
JN2738.I58 P65 2002
327.1244—dc21

                                                    2002007365

Manufactured in the United States of America

Cover image: Site of "La Piscine," the former headquarters of the DGSE in Paris, France. In 2001, the DGSE moved its headquarters to the fort of Noisy-le-Sec.

INSIDE THE WORLD'S MOST FAMOUS INTELLIGENCE AGENCIES

Contents

Introduction

Espionage is a French word that describes the act of uncovering the secret plans and activities of an enemy. It was coined in 1793, during the reign of terror that followed the overthrow of the monarchy, six years before Napoléon Bonaparte declared himself emperor of France. The term "espionage" includes spying on a country, an army, a business, a person, or any other real or imagined enemy.

The information that spies gather is called intelligence. Espionage and intelligence are controversial because they involve secret activity. People worry that intelligence gathering threatens their rights to privacy.

There are different types of intelligence for different purposes. An army commander needs military intelligence to try to predict enemy plans. A company president may want to obtain a competitor's secret designs to make a similar product. The leader of a country needs a combination of intelligence information to make knowledgeable decisions about defending his or her country.

"National security" is a phrase we have heard often, especially since the September 11, 2001, terrorist attacks on the World Trade Center in New York City and the Pentagon in Washington, D.C. It is the job of the people who work for intelligence services to help protect their nation's security by investigating threats that might lead to these kinds of attacks.

Preventing biological attacks is now one of the main responsibilities of intelligence agencies all over the world. This seemingly innocent-looking letter was opened in October 2001 in the office of U.S. Senate Majority Leader Tom Daschle. Because it contained deadly Anthrax powder, nearly fifty staff members, who may have been exposed to it, were treated with antibiotics.

The main responsibility of an intelligence agent is to uncover information that will help a country's leaders make knowledgeable decisions about their defense policies. People are motivated by different goals, so it is important to understand an opponent well enough to predict his or her actions. To do this, agents must find specific and accurate answers to many questions. How powerful is the enemy? When, where, and how might they strike? How would the enemy respond in a given situation?

A threat to a country is the possibility that an enemy will harm its people or way of life. An armed invasion, a hijacking, a kidnapping, or a bombing all pose risks to a nation's security. Nuclear weapons are powerful threats. Biological attacks, such as the letters containing anthrax spores sent to U.S. senators and handled by postal workers, are threats. Whether a threat is real or imagined, as with several anthrax false alarms, it is the job of intelligence agencies to gather information and investigate the level of danger.

People who gather intelligence are called agents or spies. Diplomats or other people whose jobs place them in good positions to hear important information can also be spies. By listening carefully to people who know details, spies uncover what is called human intelligence (abbreviated as HUMINT).

Spies also collect information electronically. This is called signals intelligence (SIGINT). Over 100 countries belong to the Intelsat communications network that links satellites above the Atlantic, Pacific, and Indian Oceans. Many nations rely on the Internet and Intelsat systems to collect signals intelligence.

Foreign intelligence is information gathered outside of a country that a government uses to protect itself against attack or injury by another country or group. Domestic intelligence is information gathered within a country. The goal of domestic intelligence is to uncover threats inside a state's borders.

Counterintelligence is used to prevent an enemy from uncovering important or sensitive information. Counterintelligence agents sometimes block enemy spies from uncovering secrets by giving them false information.

Although they use many of the same tools to gather intelligence as other countries, the French place a higher value on domestic (internal) intelligence than on foreign (external) intelligence. Because of the special pride in its language and culture, the French government has a history of treating foreigners or political opponents with suspicion for not being "French" enough. The *Economist* reported in 1999 that French leaders have equated the security of their country with homogeneity, or sameness, of its people. The French government has been known to view outsiders—especially groups living in France who identify themselves as Bretons, Basques, Corsicans, and a growing Muslim population (now the largest minority in France)—as a threat.

A policeman, in about 1940, checks the identity cards of French citizens, a common French practice, especially when there is political turmoil. Freedom of movement, threatened in the United States since the terrorist attacks of September 11, is a privilege many Americans have taken for granted.

As a result, the French government, which requires its citizens to carry identity cards, can send people to prison for up to four years without explaining the charges against them. The French government is quicker than other democratic governments to use secret microphones, telephone wiretaps, and e-mail spying on its own residents. French people tolerate, or seem to accept, restrictions that many citizens of the United States and Canada would fight.

Chapter One

How the French Secret Service Began

In 1590, after King Henri IV created the first French post office, he discovered that he could uncover revolutionary plots or useful gossip by secretly reading letters sent by soldiers and statesmen. And so began the questionable custom of reading people's mail.

Napoléon, in his quest to conquer the world, was the first to organize the sly practice of opening mail. He established the *cabinet noir* (black chamber, or secret office) to intercept the mail of anyone whose opinions he questioned. The mail checkers were especially watchful of foreigners or political opponents. Napoléon's soldiers collected this "intelligence" for internal security and to help win their war campaigns. As emperor, Napoleon ran an efficient espionage organization.

Spying by reading mail became so common that people created codes to prevent nosy readers from being able to read their letters. By the French Revolution (1789), a clever code breaker could earn a lot of money. The French foreign office, called the Quai d'Orsay (named for its street address), assembled its own staff to copy, falsify, or destroy letters the government considered dangerous.

Since maps were valuable tools, Napoléon's army sent scouts to sketch the landscape and scour towns that he

Cabinet *Noir* and the Growth of French Intelligence

The French government outlawed the practice of opening mail several times before it finally came to an end.

1789 The newly formed French National Assembly declares it illegal to tamper with mail.

1800 Cabinet noir employs code breakers, technicians, translators, and observers of "foreign" habits.

1806 Cabinet noir in Paris reads 200 letters a day of agents and diplomats.

1828 Cabinet noir is outlawed because reading people's mail was a contradiction between what the law stated as the right thing to do and what the leaders thought might insure the safety of the country and their regime.

1830 The new government cuts cabinet noir budget by one-tenth.

1848 The government eliminates cabinet noir (again).

1866 The French army employs no spies because it considers them shady.

1870 The first official French intelligence office, under the Third Republic, runs a spy service, translation bureau, and unit to question prisoners during the Franco-Prussian War. Illegal letter-checking continues, more for domestic surveillance than for addressing foreign affairs.

intended to invade. The more accurate the maps and the local intelligence, the better military leaders were able to plan their strategies.

Joseph Fouché, Duc d'Otrante (1758–1820), once a school teacher, became Napoléon's Minister of Police in 1799. Fearing that Fouché was accumulating too much power, Napoléon removed him from this office. Two years later, Napoléon appointed Fouché security chief.

In 1804, Napoléon created the Ministry of General Police, placing Joseph Fouché in charge of internal security. Fouché is given credit for developing the first modern political espionage system. Six years later, when Napoléon discovered Fouché secretly dealing with the British, he replaced him with Savary, his trusted former bodyguard. Rivalry between Fouché and Savary is said to have weakened France's ability to use intelligence information to its best advantage. And so began the tradition of strained relations between French leaders and its civil institutions. Political and military leaders have long complained that the French courts and lawmaking bodies have limited the effectiveness of French intelligence organizations.

Intelligence played a large part in Napoléon's success. He relied on a network of agents in England to uncover advance details about hiding places, travel routes, and lines of communication. But there are limits to how much even the most accurate intelligence can change the uncertainty of war, says military historian Douglas Porch in his book *The French Secret Services*. In addition to having good intelligence, Napoléon also won his battles by

"A leader has the right to be beaten but never surprised."

—Napoléon Bonaparte

trickery, by fighting weak enemies, and because the enemy missed warning signs.

French History and Politics from 1789 to 1958

In 1789, the French people began their revolution to abolish the monarchy by storming the Bastille, a gruesome French prison. Tried and convicted of treason in 1793, King Louis XVI and Queen Marie Antoinette were beheaded in Paris. Robespierre presided over the Reign of Terror (1793–1794) in France until his own execution.

In 1799, Napoléon's army entered Paris. Crowning himself emperor of the First Republic of France in 1804, Napoléon set out to conquer the rest of Europe. They advanced as far as Moscow, where they were defeated. In

This detail from a painting by Jacques-Louis David depicts the 1804 coronation of Emperor Napoléon I in the Cathedral of Notre Dame, Paris.

On July 14, 1789, a huge, bloodthirsty mob stormed a filthy, inhumane Paris prison called the Bastille. They were searching for gunpowder and prisoners who had been taken by their hated king, Louis XVI. To celebrate this event, considered the beginning of the French Revolution, the French observe Bastille Day every July 14th.

1814, when Napoléon's army lost to the British at Waterloo, he was deported to Santa Helena, an island off the coast of Africa. France acquired no land from the Napoleonic Wars, but Napoléon's administration and law left a permanent mark.

Napoléon was replaced by Louis XVIII, who ruled from 1814 to 1824. He was overthrown by Charles X, who ruled France from 1824 to 1830. Charles X was removed after the July Revolution of 1830. The July Monarchy elected a king, Louis Philippe, who headed France from 1830 to 1848.

The French middle class triumphed again in 1848, electing Louis Napoléon, nephew of Napoléon I, president of the Second Republic. In 1852, he was proclaimed Emperor Napoléon III.

During the Second Empire, France expanded its influence and prosperity in Africa and in Indochina. In 1869, Napoléon III instituted a more liberal regime by establishing a parliamentary government. But the empire ended disastrously in the Franco-Prussian War (1870–1871), in which France lost the region of Alsace-Lorraine to Germany (until 1918) and Napoléon III was exiled.

The French monarchy ended officially in 1871 when the Third Republic was proclaimed. It lasted until the Fourth Republic was established in 1946. Reorganized

Prussian troops parade on the Champs Elysees in Paris after they took over Paris during the Franco-Prussian War in January 1871. France reactivated its intelligence service at the beginning of the Franco- Prussian War.

as the French Union, the new French constitution was quite similar to that of the Third Republic. The Fourth Republic was destroyed by the war for independence in Algeria. Charles de Gaulle established the Fifth Republic and became its first president in 1958.

Why France Needed a Secret Service

Once the British defeated Napoléon in 1815, it took more than sixty years for France's intelligence organization to become active again, motivated by the start of the Franco-Prussian War. While the French government may have gathered information during this period, they had no way to interpret it. As a result, they did not know what to expect from an enemy.

In 1870, Charles de Freycinet created France's first official government intelligence office of the Third Republic to keep track of France's friends and foes. Run by a military engineer, France's first government intelligence office was split into a spy service, a translation bureau, and a unit to question prisoners of war. Surveillance, or spying, was carried out by a small group of diplomats, officers, soldiers, and police who wanted to uncover information about a possible German invasion.

Alfred Dreyfus, the French army captain who was falsely accused of stealing military secrets for Germany in 1894, is shown here with his lawyer. Dreyfus's conviction was overturned nearly twelve years later, and, according to *Time* magazine, it took until September 1995 for a representative of the French army to acknowledge in public for the first time that the army had been wrong.

The Franco-Prussian War, between France and Prussia, marked the rise of military power in Germany, which had an appetite for land. (Prussia was the most powerful state in Germany, with two-thirds of its land and people.) It was the plan of Prussian leader Otto von Bismarck to build, unite, and rule a German empire. Germany was proclaimed in 1879.

In size, efficiency, military might, or industrial strength, France was no match for a unified Germany. Once defeated by the Prussians, France had no allies, so it needed a secret service to protect its borders.

The Case That Caused a Furor

In France, Emile Zola and Marcel Proust were writers who championed Alfred Dreyfus. In 1894, Zola wrote an open letter of protest to the president of France. That letter, entitled "J'accuse," launched the campaign to free the unfairly convicted officer.

The Dreyfus Affair

A crisis in 1894, known as the Dreyfus Affair, made the French people question how far they could trust their government or its secret service. The scandal began when a French spy in the German embassy in Paris found an unsigned note with a list of France's weapons and secret troop exercises. Based on flimsy evidence, the French army accused Captain Alfred Dreyfus of spying for Germany. The fact that he was Jewish, came from Alsace-Lorraine (a region France resented losing in the war to Germany), and spoke German made him a suspect. Dreyfus proclaimed his innocence, but the French people and the press were determined to convict him.

In 1894, a court martial found Dreyfus guilty and he was banished for life to Devil's Island, off the coast of French Guiana. When it was finally revealed that the military hid information that would have proven him innocent, and the real culprit was a well-connected officer by the name of Esterhazi, Dreyfus was cleared of all charges. In 1906, after twelve years, Dreyfus was finally pardoned by the French court.

The Dreyfus Affair captured the attention of reporters and concerned citizens, raising questions about democratic principles. People began to think about the rights of citizens and the integrity of government. What can protect citizens against abuses of power? How independent are the civil and military codes of justice? Some of the lessons about justice learned in the Dreyfus Affair have lasted.

How France Defines and Defends Its Interests

The Dreyfus case revealed the undercurrents of French prejudice and patriotic fanaticism. Yet this was not the first time France acted out of fear of being betrayed by an "outsider," a person considered "not French enough," living and working inside a French institution.

From its early history, France has spent more energy on domestic intelligence, gathering information about suspicious activity within its borders, than on tracking threats from outside the country.

In 1906, France's prime minister (and interior minister) Georges Clemenceau expanded the scope of government surveillance. Foreigners were accustomed to being questioned. But now national and religious minorities, and people living in French colonies, also became the targets of investigation. The government reasoned that if France was free from outside influence, French citizens could enjoy safety and political freedom at home. But at what cost would that be to privacy and to human rights? History tells us that the Dreyfus Affair marked the peak of distrust in the French secret service.

Chapter Two

French Intelligence Today

Today, two government agencies protect the people of France from outside threats, real or imagined. The French foreign intelligence agency, DGSE, or Direction Générale de la Sécurité Exterieure (General Directorate of External Security), takes charge of military and electronic intelligence, strategic information, and counterespionage beyond France's borders. The military intelligence agency, DRM, or Direction du Renseignement Militaire (Directorate of Military Intelligence), plans, coordinates, and leads military intelligence investigations within France's borders. Both agencies report to the French ministry of defense. Although they are based in Paris, half of France's 4,200 secret service agents are stationed in other countries. Many agents work under diplomatic cover.

Until 1999, the military ran the French intelligence agency. Then, for the first time in France's history, a diplomat took the lead. Jean-Claude Cousseran was former ambassador to Turkey and a strategist in the French foreign service, also called the Quai d'Orsay. Cousseran reorganized the agency to improve the flow of information. He appointed specialists to work closely with the DGSE departments of strategy, analysis, operations, technology, and administration. These nine men and women have greatly improved communication throughout the agency.

Where Is France?

France is located southeast of and across the English Channel from Great Britain, between Belgium and Spain. It is bordered by the Bay of Biscay on the west. Sitting between Italy and Spain, France is bound by the Mediterranean Sea on the southeast and Germany in the northeast. The largest nation in western Europe, France (excluding its overseas territories) is roughly twice the size of Colorado.

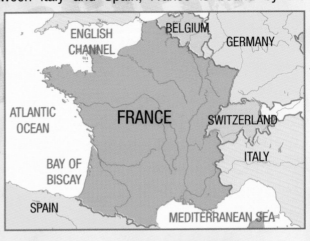

The top priority of the DGSE is to inform the French president and prime minister of critical intelligence. Agents sort the raw intelligence before a government panel reviews and directs it to the right department. Experts say this had long been the bottleneck, or source of delays, at the DGSE.

Now and Then

In 1992, most of the defense responsibilities of the DGSE from the Cold War (the 1950s to 1991) were transferred to the Military Intelligence Directorate (DRM), a new military intelligence agency. Combining the skills and knowledge of five military groups, the DRM was created to close the intelligence gaps of the 1991 Gulf War. The Center for Military Intelligence Exploitation is its smallest and most secretive intelligence unit. Other DRM units include Electromagnetic Radiation, Imagery Interpretation, and the Inter-Army Helios Unit, a division of the army and air force.

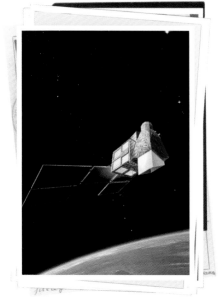

In 1999, France launched the *Helios 1B* satellite. An improved all-weather version of the four-year-old *Helios 1A* satellite, the new craft can take intelligence photographs in the dark, but still cannot see through clouds, which often block its view of the earth.

DRM headquarters are in Paris, with technical groups in Creil (in Oise, a northern region). The DRM collects human and electronic intelligence, and analyzes satellite and electromagnetic images, which it shares with its former enemy, Germany. The agency also studies and analyzes threats about the spread of nuclear technology and chemical and other weapons. The DRM recruits and trains intelligence workers to provide the agency with technical support.

Since 1992, the DRM's duties have expanded from supplying purely military intelligence to gathering information that affects national policy and strategy. This job had been the chief responsibility of the DGSE.

Satellite Communications

The International Telecommunications Satellite Organization, or Intelsat, is a communications network above the Atlantic, Pacific, and Indian Oceans that links together 110 countries.

Inmarsat supplies mobile satellite services which enable people to communicate over 210,000 terminals on ships, planes, and other vehicles.

In 1995, half of the 2,000-person staff of the DRM came from France's army. One-quarter of the staff represented the air force. The rest of the staff of the DRM was composed of equal parts navy and civil service workers, plus a small number of police. That same year, the DRM began reporting to the defense ministry in place of the army. The soldiers who once staffed the DGSE now work for the DRM.

The DRM oversees the Helios space observation program. Since August 1995, the Helios satellite has taken high-definition photographs that are used to help protect France from conflict. However, a French news source learned that the agency hid a cartridge on board the satellite to intercept Inmarsat and Intelsat civilian communication signals.

The French have also launched French surveillance stations. While the DGSE is a secret service, the DRM is not. Its responsibility is research, not internal security.

Keeping in Step with Change

Since the gravest threats to security keep changing, the DRM keeps up with new challenges by recruiting experts who have mastered the tools of self-defense. The agency needs people who are skilled with analysis, language, and technology to prepare political and economic reports as well as to gather information that will help France fight terrorism, organized crime, and the spread of weapons of mass destruction.

Both branches of the French intelligence agency are better known for their technical skills than for their human intelligence (HUMINT) network. Together, the DGSE and DMR created an advanced electronic spy network that the government kept secret until February 2000, when the newspaper *Le Monde* published a list of surveillance bases. The DGSE runs signals intelligence (SIGINT) operations from ground stations for long-range monitoring of spy ships and aircraft.

The French secret service budget increases each year to allow France to expand its network of satellites and to extend its "listening" range. *Jane's Intelligence Review* estimated the total intelligence agency budget in France in 2000 at $1 billion. Half the budget went to diplomatic and political efforts, while the rest was divided equally between military and economic expenses.

France has established ten stations in its overseas territories and former colonies. From sites in the West Indies, Corsica, Africa, Mayotte (in the Indian Ocean), and New Caledonia (in the South Pacific Ocean), the agency monitors countless telephone, e-mail, and fax communications.

The Secret to France's "Supersonic" Ears

Taïga is the name of software that runs on powerful supercomputers to automatically sort geopolitical information from current events. Most cryptography programs work by identifying key words. Taïga is different because it analyzes the root of a word. Developed in 1987 by linguist Christian Krumeich, Taïga can search for information through an avalanche of news in any language.

In June 2000, Zdnet.UK.com reported on an agreement between France and the United Arab Emirates that permits French surveillance stations in the Persian Gulf state. And the French secretly planted equipment on the space station *Kourou,* shared by the German secret service, that monitors satellite transmissions in the Americas.

Satellites track electronic signals and can be programmed to identify different characteristics. According to *Le Nouvel Observateur,* a French newsweekly, the largest satellites check the Internet and e-mail systems. Other satellites monitor specific regions. For example, Arabsat monitors communications in the Middle East.

France can capture, copy, and circulate any communication—within France or to another country—without permission from anyone. Of all the countries in the Western world, only France does this because its government makes such a hazy distinction between foreign, domestic, public, and private information.

What Was "the Pool?"

Why was "the Pool" (*piscine*) slang for the French secret service? Because the DGSE office was located next to an enormous public swimming pool on the outskirts of Paris.

The Great Challenge of Breaking Codes

The French secret services are known for using unusual ways to break codes. In addition to negotiating or using bribes to obtain computer disks with stored information, agents sometimes steal them. When all else fails, French code breakers must use time-consuming trial and error methods.

With 200 people working at the DGSE center in Bordeaux (near the western coast of France), 200 people in Paris, and 40 people in Mayotte (in the Indian Ocean), teams of technicians decode the intercepted messages.

Operators comb telephone conversations and e-mail for keywords, making lists of people and words to watch for. "Pearls"—information of great value—are rare. People's handwriting and accents make faxes and telephone conversations the hardest to decode and the least reliable.

Chapter Three

Intelligence and the Fall of France

Predicting an enemy's actions is an intelligence agency's *raison d'être* ("reason for being"). Leaders in government or battle must review the intelligence information before choosing a plan of action.

Intelligence in Wartime

How did the French predict Germany's actions in World Wars I and II? The planning and outcome of two important events are revealing.

World War I

In August 1914, World War I broke out in Europe. Tensions had mushroomed into feuds between France and Germany, between Germany and Britain, and between Russia and Austria-Hungary. France needed to arm and train many soldiers in a hurry.

On the eve of war, Germany had strength, but France had military intelligence. For the first time, air reconnaissance and radio and telephone technology made it possible to transmit "real time" information. Being able to communicate on the spot made it possible to influence the outcome of a battle.

French soldiers knew a great deal about servicing their aircraft, but they knew woefully little about the realities of fighting a war. Most of their limited field training came from an orange booklet titled "What You Need to Know About the German Army."

The Schlieffen Plan

France's most argued-over prewar success was to attain a secret German war

General Alfred von Schlieffen formulated Germany's attack on France through Belgium in World War I.

plan that practically fell into the hands of French intelligence. Called the Schlieffen Plan, this document proved to be the basis for Germany's opening attack on France in August 1914. A German officer had sold it to the French war ministry in exchange for 60,000 francs, which was a huge sum at the time. The work of German chief of staff Count Alfred von Schlieffen, the plan described an attack of twenty-six army corps that would march into France through Belgium. Their goal was to conquer Paris within six weeks, as happened in 1879.

French agents, seeing military troop practice in 1906, suspected that the Germans planned to surround France by marching through Belgium. This was confirmed by details in the Schlieffen Plan. Still, French commander in chief Joseph

French commander Marshall Joseph Joffre (1852–1931) is shown here in 1930 as he leaves the Park Hotel in London. Joffre persisted in his plan to fight the Germans rather than rethink it once he received new information about enemy moves.

Joffre made a counterplan to lead the French armies northeast into Alsace-Lorraine.

Despite the intelligence he had, Joffre was completely surprised by the German attack in August 1914. As German troop strength mounted, the Belgians petitioned Joffre for help. Still, Joffre ignored the growing threat. Told the whereabouts of sixteen of the twenty-six German troops, he assumed the missing ten were far from Belgium. He was wrong.

Did French intelligence misunderstand the Schlieffen Plan, as some historians have said? Or was Joffre so intent on doing things his way that he refused to believe the new facts and change his strategy?

While French intelligence agents suspected Germany would descend on France from Belgium, it appears that Joffre refused to believe them. Joffre and his command made two fatal mistakes. They underestimated the strength of the German army, and they didn't foresee the western arc of the German army advancing toward Paris.

The Germans, on the contrary, knew exactly what to expect of the French army. They had attained a copy of Joffre's troop movement schedule and an outline of his counterplan.

General Henri Navarre, who spent his career in and wrote about military intelligence, blamed Joffre for ignoring not one but many intelligence alarms. Joffre, who discounted German plans to reinforce their reserve units, rejected reports of Germany's superior heavy artillery and new weapons, including toxic gases. Navarre argued that Joffre ignored the Belgian route described in the Schlieffen Plan because it clashed with his concept of what the enemy had in mind.

History Repeats Itself in WW II

Long after the Dreyfus Affair, military intelligence in France continued to be ineffectual because it was revamped with every new administration. There was no well-established central organization to manage the crush of information coming from many sources.

As the Germans began to attack Europe in 1939, French secret service agents were scattered around France, and counterespionage was transferred to the office of interior ministry. Officers were appointed to the hastily organized, tiny new service. Five officers at headquarters collected intelligence on Italy and Austria from officers located at three regional posts. Agents in four additional posts kept tabs on Germany. But no one was assigned the job of watching Belgium, even though this was the route the Germans took in World War I as they marched on Paris in 1914.

The French army had trouble using intelligence to create a unified picture of the enemy. And so did the leaders of France's divided political system.

Map of French and German Plans for the Battle of France 1940

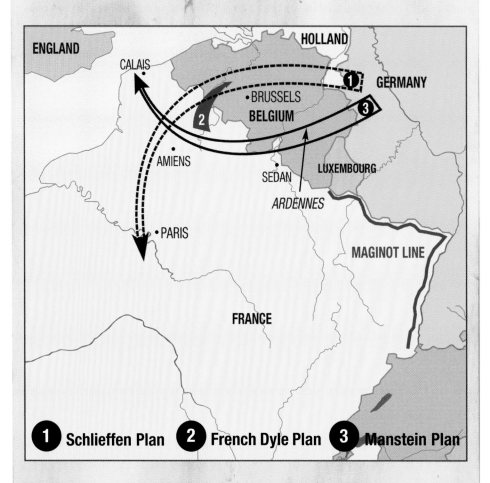

ENGLAND

HOLLAND

CALAIS

GERMANY

1

•BRUSSELS

2

3

BELGIUM

AMIENS

SEDAN

LUXEMBOURG

ARDENNES

•PARIS

MAGINOT LINE

FRANCE

1 Schlieffen Plan 2 French Dyle Plan 3 Manstein Plan

The French expected the Germans to attack them following a route similar to the one used during World War I, described in the Schlieffen Plan, so they created an updated version called the Dyle Plan. Instead, the Germans attacked from the south and overpowered the unprepared French.

Why Didn't the French Stop Hitler in 1940?

After Germany attacked Poland, it was a matter of when and where Hitler would strike France. Allied commander Maurice Gamelin decided to splinter his headquarters, which made it harder for important intelligence to reach commanders. Motorcyclists in goggles ferried satchels of communiqués back and forth, day and night, between five locations.

Gamelin (who had served under Joffre in World War I) also divided his intelligence staff. Half accompanied him east of Paris to Vincennes. The rest stayed in the war ministry, close to the prime minister. Torn between the commander in chief and the minister of national defense, the service didn't know whom to obey.

One lone intelligence agent held down headquarters. In May 1940, he watched over the teletype as it rattled out pages of information so conflicting he called it the "fiction flood."

That same month, the intelligence bureau set up quarters in a vacant chateau twenty-five miles from Paris. A cluster of cryptographers were encamped nearby. However, most of the code breakers stayed behind in Paris to decode telegrams that never came. Meanwhile, General Gamelin, who had the final power of decision, remained in Vincennes.

To add to the problems of inexperienced soldiers, German planes blocked a French air reconnaissance mission. Because Gamelin's men were scattered, it was difficult for the French to communicate with each other over their radios. Deciding which intelligence was priceless and which was worthless took precious hours. And General Gamelin was miles away in Vincennes.

At the outbreak of World War II, General Maurice Gamelin *(right)* assured his government that France had the most powerful army in the world. After splintering his command, making it difficult to communicate with or mobilize his troops, he was shocked when the French army was easily defeated. Gamelin was relieved of his position in May 1940.

Coordinating and verifying intelligence was especially complicated because of the scattered organization. In addition, General Gamelin did not fully trust the information he received from intelligence agents about the dangers ahead.

Where Would Germany Attack?

Gamelin and the Allies expected Germany to strike roughly where they had in World War I: West and north through Belgium, then south toward Paris (following the Schlieffen Plan). So the French created the Dyle Plan to stop the German forces in north Belgium.

Gamelin's goals were to save French lives, enlist allies against a stronger foe, and protect French territory. But this

An American Spy in Paris

During World War II, Virginia Hall, a young woman from Baltimore, went to work for the French as an agent. She was so successful that the Nazis began to search for her. In the winter of 1941, just when they were about to arrest her, she escaped on foot, over the Pyrenees Mountains, into Spain. This was no easy task, for she had lost her leg in a hunting accident and wore a wooden leg at the time of her escape. Not content to rest, she trained to be a radio operator and transferred to America's Office of Special Services. She returned to France before the war ended to continue her espionage duties.

plan took the risk of pushing French forces too far into Belgium and leaving French soil wide open to attack. If the Germans came through the Ardennes, it would be hard for French troops to resist them. The Dyle Plan would have left them defenseless, but Gamelin would not listen to reason.

Gamelin's commanding officers all agreed that it was dangerous to tempt Germany to cut them off. But not even Gamelin's own men could convince him of the risks. The worst problem was that Belgium's defenses were weak. Gamelin would need help from Belgium for his plan to succeed.

The Dyle Plan Backfires

But on May 10, 1940, French air reconnaissance did not detect German preparations on the front. The Germans, on the other hand, knew exactly what the French expected

During World War II, Germany occupied France from 1940 to 1944. In this photograph, shot in 1940, German troops ride through Paris. The Arc de Triomphe is visible behind them.

because they had a copy of France's Dyle Plan. In addition, Germany had mastered a technique of gradually and secretly moving forces to the battle line, troop by troop, to launch a surprise attack.

The Dyle Plan sent France's limited reconnaissance planes into Belgium, leaving the armies in the Ardennes without cover. German troops cut a wide arc around the French as they moved south through Belgium and west through the Ardennes forest. Then they swung north to the English Channel.

On May 14, a shift in French air forces ended in slaughter when the Germans mowed down the French troops isolated in the Ardennes.

This photo, from August 28, 1944, shows French general Charles de Gaulle during the celebrations after American troops liberated Paris from the Germans. Having just left the Arc de Triomphe, de Gaulle was headed to the Place de la Concorde.

What Went Wrong?

Did Germany prevent French intelligence from getting the information it needed? Or was it a losing battle for French intelligence and military officers to challenge the fixed ideas of the French high command? Historian Douglas Porch says in *The French Secret Services* that, at the start of World War II, France's intelligence was far more advanced than Germany's. But in the end, Gamelin, like Joffre, insisted on following his original plan in spite of French intelligence warning him against it. Once again, French military leaders appear to have stubbornly ignored important intelligence information. To their frustration, French intelligence officials could not put their findings to good use because military leaders would not listen to their well-informed perspective.

The Germans invaded Paris in 1940 and occupied the north and west of France until 1944. Meanwhile, a puppet government was set up in the town of Vichy, led by Marshal Petain. However, General Charles de Gaulle organized a resistance movement to keep France independent of Germany.

On June 6, 1944, now known as D-Day, Allied forces invaded the beaches of Normandy to defeat Germany in World War II. Germany, weak from being bombed around the clock and starved by the Allied blockade, finally surrendered to the Western Allies on May 8, 1945. De Gaulle entered Paris to head the new government of the Fifth Republic.

Chapter Four

The End of an Empire

Since the nineteenth century, France had built a huge empire abroad. France prospered by trading goods with its colonies in Africa and Indochina in exchange for raw materials and crops. Before 1860, France had occupied Algeria, Vietnam, and several islands in the Pacific. But after World War II, France began to feel resistance as its territories struggled for independence.

Dien Bien Phu

One of the most closely dissected battles in history took place in Dien Bien Phu, Vietnam, on what was then a French military base.

Since the end of World War II, the French had occupied pockets of Indochina, which consisted of present-day Vietnam, Cambodia, and Laos, and were accustomed to fighting off guerrilla forces. In November 1953, the French parachuted into the hills of Dien Bien Phu to block Vietnamese forces, the Viet Minh, from crossing the border into Laos. The French, weakened by past disasters, were convinced that their base was safe from attack because they thought it could be reached only by air.

Meanwhile, General Vo Nguyen Giap planned to lead the Viet Minh in a revolution in northern Vietnam to overwhelm the French. With the help of communist China, Vietnam's powerful

In November 1953, French paratroopers watched as more French troops parachuted into Dien Bien Phu. While the French were able to capture this enemy stronghold, in the end they were defeated by the Viet Minh.

ally (who knew France was determined to protect the local French-led forces, who were deriving profits from their opium trade), the Viet Minh quietly trained and gathered strength. China was happy to weaken a Western power as the Korean War it fought with the U.S. was ending. By spring 1954, 50,000 Viet Minh fighters silently moved heavy artillery through the jungle and surrounded Dien Bien Phu from the delta below.

French intelligence kept Commander Henri Navarre informed of the enemy's troop movements by listening to Viet Minh radio communications, although they could not predict their strategy. You might think a French military leader would have recalled that this was the same technique the Germans had used in World War II. But no one did. As a result, the Viet Minh assault devastated Navarre's troops. Fifty-six days later, the French were outnumbered three to one.

France's underestimating—or refusing to see—the Viet Minh's ability to overwhelm them at Dien Bien Phu led to a failure that historian Douglas Porch claims in *The French Secret Services* "changed the course of French history." One problem was that Navarre's plan never took into account enemy intentions or capabilities. Historian Porch compares this to earlier French defeats under Generals Joffre (1914) and Gamelin (1940). He asks who is responsible for persuading leaders to take a particular course of action. Who should decide how to balance what is certain against perceived domestic capabilities and those of the enemy: intelligence or legislature?

Algeria

France pulled out of Indochina to concentrate on quieting a revolt in Algeria, a French possession closer to home. Explosions in Algiers, the capital, in November 1954 once again took the French government by surprise. Interior Minister Francois Mitterand (who became president of France in 1981) demanded to know why he hadn't been warned. The director of the internal intelligence agency, the DST, told him that the police in Algeria and France had reported their discovery of arms, propaganda for independence, and plans for a revolt against French rule in North Africa. But the report had been gathering dust for eight months. Still, French authorities held back a plan to destroy the rebel network.

Resentment against the French had been growing slowly since the French lost to Germany in 1940. By 1954, Algeria had reached a critical point. But France seemed to miss all the signs.

French intelligence tried and failed to stop Ahmed Ben Bella, a leader of rebel forces in Algeria.

French intelligence targeted Ahmed Ben Bella, a founder of the Algerian Front for National Liberation (FLN), for trading arms with and building financial support for the rebels. A French assassination team shot at Ben Bella (who was a decorated French army veteran)—and missed. To add insult to injury, the secret service missed again in 1956, when a bomb planted outside his office left Ben Bella unharmed.

Not discouraged after two strikes, French intelligence then learned that Ben Bella was to fly to Tunisia to meet with Arab and FLN leaders. The French defense ministry ordered a French air force pilot to hijack Ben Bella's plane and take him back to Algeria.

Ben Bella's capture turned into a disaster. The response to the violation of international laws was widespread outrage. The French government was embarrassed. French diplomats resigned. Anti-French riots erupted in Morocco. To this day, no

"Without Allied intelligence, we were almost blind."
——French Defense Minister Pierre Joxe

government authority has claimed responsibility for ordering the operation.

The president of Tunisia, Habib Bourgiba, and the king of Morocco, Muhummad V, were ready to negotiate peace, but the kidnap and arrest of Ben Bella ended any chance of diplomatic settlement between the French and the FLN.

The secret service tactics—assassinations, bombings, hijackings—simply mirrored the army's approach to the Algerian problem. Once again, action took the place of strategy. By not considering how their opponent might respond, the French insulted Arab leaders and ruined the chance of compromise. By 1970, France had lost nearly all of its overseas possessions.

The Gulf War

From 1958 to the 1980s, under governments that put loyalty above truth or effectiveness, the reputation of the French intelligence service grew gradually worse. Intelligence was being used too often as a weapon rather than as a tool to set strategy or influence policy. One major example was the 1985 bombing of the *Rainbow Warrior*, a ship used by environmental activists to monitor French nuclear experiments in the Pacific Ocean.

By the time the Gulf War broke out in 1991, the French intelligence structure had become fragmented, understaffed, and ignored. Early in the crisis, a French officer had warned President Mitterand that France would pay for its outdated policy of using tanks and ships rather than satellites to gather intelligence information.

These French military vehicles, which are painted in desert camouflage, were transported in 1990 to the battlefields of the Gulf War. Although the French had limited intelligence capabilities, they were able to capture and contribute data from air surveillance and intercepted radio signals.

And pay it did. Mitterand learned about the Iraqi buildup in the Persian Gulf from an American admiral who had satellite photos to prove it. When Mitterand's request to keep the photos for his own experts to interpret was denied, the French president was faced with a difficult truth: French intelligence could not produce vital information. The 150-member staff of the Centre d'Exploitation du Renseignement Militaire, or CERM (Center for Use of Military Information), was too small and poorly equipped to advise the high command.

The less prepared France felt, the more suspicious it was about having to depend on the United States. (Mitterand was convinced the United States had foreseen Saddam Hussein's plan to invade Kuwait. In fact, neither the United States nor Israel foresaw it.) However, this may be why Mitterand shifted

Why France Failed to Use Intelligence Intelligently

- France was often held back by a bureaucracy where many services worked in secrecy from each other.
- The military command did not often welcome outside points of view.
- French intelligence agents developed technological knowledge but were unable to use the information effectively.

his support restlessly from Saddam back to the West. Then the Americans launched Operation: Desert Storm in January 1991.

The French did contribute battlefield intelligence from air surveillance and radio interception, working with a CERM ship and with Arabic translators. But its small staff was taxed to the limit.

The Painful Truth

The Gulf War crisis made France painfully aware of the need to rethink its foreign intelligence priorities. Its leaders had to accept that its intelligence services could not support its ambitions. The DGSE knew, despite its efforts, that it was not equipped to supply global intelligence. France's intelligence organization was long overdue for reform.

The first step was to coordinate the work of several agencies and invest in military intelligence equipment, including

The DGSE bombing of the first *Rainbow Warrior* resulted in a serious diplomatic crisis and embarrassed French president Mitterand.

electronic surveillance. A new Interministerial Intelligence Committee (CIR) brought together concerned ministers with the heads of the French domestic intelligence service, the Direction de la Surveillance du Territoire (DST), and the DGSE. In 1992, the Military Intelligence Directorate (DRM) was created to bring order to the services groups. The DRM also took responsibility from the DGSE for coordinating special action missions. Once again the military was put in charge of correcting the same old problems: poor internal coordination and communication. And again this raised the question, How does a government protect the state and respect the rights of its citizens?

The legendary Action Service of the DGSE, like the U.S. Green Beret special forces, now has 300 agents stationed at a secret base near Orléans, France. This group is smaller than it was in 1985, when it sank the Greenpeace ship, the *Rainbow Warrior.*

A newsletter for ex-U.S. intelligence agents reports that French DGSE workers complain that the DST is cramping their style. The 1,500-member DST police force was once in charge of counterintelligence. Now their job is to track foreign criminals and terrorists operating in France.

Chapter Five

France Looks Ahead

Since the Gulf War in 1991, France has increased its use of communications technology to protect its borders and defend its governing principles. Military matters still count, but now the focus of intelligence has turned toward dangers in new realms.

The nature of threats and enemies are becoming more complicated. The lines between internal and external threats and between national boundaries have become blurred. And the ways to fight them—including the use of Internet and satellite technology—have become much more advanced.

France's National Prestige

According to America's Central Intelligence Agency (CIA), when France lost its empire, it also lost its wealth, manpower, and rank as a nation, despite its place among the Allies in World Wars I and II. Yet France today is a leader among European nations. The French government, now a presidential democracy, has been more stable in the last fifty years than it was as a parliamentary democracy.

France's newfound cooperation with Germany has helped cement the economic integration of Europe, including the adoption of the euro (1999) as the common currency for members of the European Union. France is trying to expand that sense of solidarity to create a stronger, more unified system of European defense.

Member nations of the European Union have agreed to use the euro as their monetary standard. The euro was worth just less than a dollar (97 cents) in July 2002.

Who Is Listening . . . ?

France has repeatedly accused the United States and Great Britain of using their joint electronic surveillance, Echelon, the world's largest electronic intelligence network, to gather information about French industry. France also claims that the European Parliament first learned of this in 1998. The accusations have flown back and forth since then, making this an ongoing feud over industrial espionage. By prying information electronically, France said, the United States and Great Britain were able to help their businesses better compete in the global marketplace.

Then, in June 1998, a French newsweekly announced that France was also operating a global spy network. They dubbed it Frenchelon.

The World Is Listening

The United States and Great Britain operate Echelon to pool the security resources of the United States, Great Britain, Canada, Australia, and New Zealand to monitor and protect their populations.

The European Parliament, the governing body for matters that concern member countries of the European Union, first learned about Echelon in January 1998. In addition, Russia and Israel run worldwide listening networks. Thirty other countries—including Denmark, the Netherlands, and Switzerland—also use SIGINT (signals intelligence) to eavesdrop on selected telephone and e-mail conversations. So does France.

Where and How France Seeks Intelligence

The chief of the French defense ministry told the magazine *Le Point* that the French use "Frenchelon" for international military matters, to combat terrorism, and to prevent the spread of nonconventional weapons. *Le Point* added that France also eavesdrops on Intelsat and Inmarsat civilian communications satellites.

Listening posts on three continents capture transmissions in space and translate signals from thirty spy antennae planted around the world. Stations on the island of New Caledonia and in the United Arab Emirates cover Asia and the Middle East. Caribbean bases pick up conversations in the United States. The central station in Bordeaux, France, targets satellites over the Atlantic and Indian Oceans. Stations also monitor the skies over French Guiana and the airwaves

During July 2000 debates in the European parliament, a weary Italian Eurodeputy, Roberto Felice Bigliardo, wears a T-shirt protesting Echelon. This U.S. surveillance system is thought to sift through millions of phone calls, faxes, and e-mails every day.

of Paris. The French news magazine *Le Nouvel Observateur* declared that no one is safe from this web of "prying ears," not even countries on friendly terms with France.

France has been spying in this manner for nearly thirty years. But unlike other countries in the West, France has no laws to protect the privacy of its citizens from government intrusion. French law allows criminal suspects to be wiretapped. The messages DGSE intercepts, however, are not subject to that law.

Le Nouvel Observateur called this spying technique "a gross infringement of privacy [that is] tolerated by law." It ended by asking readers, "Other countries have measures to control spying. Why not France?"

Security vs. Liberty

"France is far from sharing American or British concerns over the potential damages of parliamentary accountability and openness. France simply has no history of proper communication between intelligence services and legislative power."

—Jean-Marc Pennetier, French intelligence journalist

To Cooperate or to Cross Swords?

France is not alone, of course, in wanting to fight terrorism and industrial espionage. And this raises another question: Should France cooperate or compete with countries fighting the same battles?

In the past, from lack of trust or interest, French leaders pushed intelligence aside in decision making. As politicians began to realize the importance of gathering intelligence, they voted their support through budget increases. Still, French presidents from de Gaulle to Chirac have viewed intelligence as a grudging bow to America, whose aid they simultaneously need and resent.

Where Should Government Draw the Line?

The way a government conducts intelligence, as we have seen, affects the way the country runs and the way people lead their lives. The French have an expression, *raison d'état*, for pride and patriotism in their country, its language, and its culture. It means what is right for the state or nation.

The French government protects the national good above personal freedoms. Governments of democracies around the world strive to balance the needs for national security and the principle of individual liberty.

The toughest issue for France may be facing up to change. France seems to be reevaluating its past and its place in the world today. Reconsidering its strengths may show France how best to protect its interests.

The Springtime of French Intelligence

France and the United States

Until January 1999, France had the strictest cryptography controls in the Western world. But a group of technologists joined with 200 companies and trade associations to convince the government to relax regulations or risk losing privacy and e-commerce trade.

Some French officials think the goal of this change was to counteract the threat of Echelon and to block the United States from intercepting French government information and trade secrets.

Easing this law was a turning point in the global debate over government control of scrambling data so that only the intended recipient can read it. Law enforcement and intelligence agencies around the world have argued to restrict encryption. High-tech firms and privacy advocates claim it is vital for electronic commerce and to the protection of privacy.

If everyone uses cryptography, it becomes harder for intelligence organizations to do their job. They scoop zillions of bits of data every day and run filters looking for clues to danger. The more strict the encryption, the harder it is to sift through.

Law enforcement would like to have a "key" to crack a code, even if it required police to physically flip a decoding switch. Businesses and defenders of privacy oppose this option.

France and Europe are driven to develop surveillance technology and protect information with encryption technology as one way to compete with and guard against America's abilities to snoop. While France is suspicious of the U.S. government, the two countries continue working together to enforce the law in certain areas, such as fighting high-tech crime and protecting encryption, or coding, technology. As surveillance continues, international discussions proceed. And neither side knows if it can trust the other.

Rivalry and Signs of Change

Espionage and intelligence go hand in hand. In the early 1990s, France rejected an FBI plan to develop an international terrorist database. France has also criticized the United States for global spying and for intelligence operations that compromised the privacy of French citizens and companies, although the French probably wouldn't think twice about doing it themselves. Nevertheless, there is always the chance, or fear, that someone from another country will discover a detail about French state secrets or commerce that a

French president Jacques Chirac and U.S. president George W. Bush met at the White House in November 2001 to discuss the crisis after the September 11 terrorist attacks on the United States.

competitor would find useful. On the other hand, Washington, D.C., and Paris have shared important information on such sensitive countries as Algeria, Iraq, and Iran.

Is France seriously rewriting its intelligence-gathering policies? Is it trying to be realistic about how it fits in the world community of the twenty-first century? Recent news items show France exploring the tradeoffs between independence, cooperation, and competition.

France's top antiterrorism official, Judge Jean-Louis Bruguière, proposed that it was a mistake for the West to focus on Osama bin Laden as the key to ending terrorism. *USA Today* reported that Judge Bruguière recommended instead that America trace thousands of people that he felt should be suspects. Until the catastrophe of September 11, this had been a clear difference between France and the rest of the West, where the law considers each person innocent until proven guilty. By law, the French can jail and detain anyone on suspicion for four years without giving him or her a reason. The French judge was suggesting we lock up any "suspicious-looking" person—for any reason. But he also imagined that the investigation would be held back by U.S. constitutional limits that French investigators don't have to overcome. At this writing, however, it appears that the United States is taking the judge's advice seriously.

Germany is reported to contribute money in return for access to the information gathered by Frenchelon, the French surveillance network. Is this another step in reconciling with Germany or an effort to counter U.S. spying capabilities?

The *New York Times* ran a front-page story about tightening security in Saudi Arabia for the annual *hajj*, or religious

Jean-Louis Bruguière, the highest-ranking antiterrorism official in France, traveled by train from Paris to Brussels on September 17, 2001, to discuss European action against terrorism with magistrates from Germany, Belgium, and Holland after the September 11 attacks in the United States.

pilgrimage, that every able Muslim must make once in a lifetime. The Saudi government documented each passport with matching digital eye scans and fingerprints to keep pilgrims safe. A French firm, hired by the U.S. Postal Service and the New York Police Department, was in charge of taking travelers' fingerprints at passport control.

It should be fascinating to watch what the French intelligence service does next in a world where the rules are constantly changing. That's what makes the future both frightening and promising—sometimes in equal measure.

Glossary

anti-Semitism   Hostility toward Jews based on perceived ethnic and cultural character.

blockade   Closing off a city or port to traffic or communication.

cabinet noir   "Black chamber," the office in charge of intercepting and reading mail and translating secret codes when necessary.

civil institutions   Organizations that govern ordinary community life, as opposed to military or religious bodies.

Cold War   The intense rivalry that developed after World War II between groups of Communist and non-Communist nations.

counterintelligence   Branch of an intelligence service in charge of keeping important or sensitive information away from an enemy, sometimes by spreading incorrect information.

cryptography   The art of writing in or deciphering secret code.

decipher   To convert (break or translate) coded messages into plain, readable text.

diplomat   A person appointed to represent his or her country with other governments.

diplomatic cover Work performed in secret, often on assignment as a diplomat working in another country.

domestic intelligence Information about secretive plans or activities inside a country that would endanger its security.

encryption Coding messages to protect them from being read.

espionage The act of getting information secretively, particularly military, industrial, and political data about one nation for the benefit of another. Industrial espionage is the theft of patents and processes from business firms.

external intelligence Information about a foreign government's plans and activities that would endanger the investigating country. It is gathered outside the borders of the investigating country

FLN Front de Libération Nationale, an Algerian organization formed to fight for independence from France.

human intelligence (HUMINT) Human- or agent-generated intelligence.

inside intelligence Information about secretive plans or activities gathered inside a country that would endanger that country.

integrity The upholding of a set of values.

intercept To stop or interrupt the progress of something; to capture a letter or message and secretly read it before it reaches its destination.

intrusion To come in rudely or unwanted.

nonconventional Out of the ordinary, as applied to weapons, including nuclear, biological, and chemical weapons.

patriotism Pride in one's country; nationalism.

Quai d'Orsay   The French foreign office.

reconcile   To reestablish a friendship after a dispute.

reconnaissance   A survey of a region's terrain (land) to determine where to place military forces.

restrictions   Limits.

rivalry   Competition.

signals intelligence (SIGINT)   Information that is collected electronically.

surveillance   Close observation, especially of a person or group under suspicion. To watch secretly.

undercurrent   A current below the surface that is sometimes quite different from what can be easily seen.

United Arab Emirates   Federation of seven sheikdoms in southeastern Arabia on the shores of the Persian Gulf: Abu Dhabi (the largest), Ajman, Dubai, Fujairah, Ras al-Khaimah, Sharjah, and Umm al-Qaiwain.

For More Information

Organizations

Amnesty International USA
National Office
322 8th Avenue
New York, NY 1001
(212) 807-8400
Web site:http://www.amnesty-usa.org

Centre for the Study of Terrorism and Political Violence
Department of International Relations
University of St. Andrews
St. Andrews, Scotland KY16 9AL
United Kingdom
Web site: http://www.stand.ac.uk/academic/intrel/
    research/cstpv

Federation of American Scientists
1717 K Street NW, Suite 209
Washington, DC 20036
(202) 546-3300
e-mail: fas@fas.org
Web site: http://www.fas.org

General Directorate for External Security
Ministère de la Défense
BCAC-CG n°196
14 rue St Dominique
00449 Armees
France

Greenpeace
702 H Street NW, Suite 300
Washington, DC 20001
1-800-326-0959
Web site: www.greenpeace.org

International Spy Museum
800 F Street
Washington, DC 20002
Web site: http://www.spymuseum.org

National Cryptologic Museum
(301) 688-5849
Web site: http://www.nsa.gov/museum/

National Security Agency (NSA)
Public Affairs Office
98 Savage Road
Fort George G. Meade, MD 20755-6779

Terrorist Group Profiles
Dudley Knox Library
Naval Post Graduate School
411 Dyer Road
Monterey, CA 93943
Web site: http://web.nps.navy.mil/~library/tgp/tgp2.htm

Web Sites

Due to the changing nature of Internet links, the Rosen
Publishing Group, Inc., has developed an online list of Web
sites related to the subject of this book. This site is
updated regularly. Please use this link to access the list:

http://www.rosenlinks.com/iwmfia/dgse/

For Further Reading

Cretzmeyer, Stacy. *Your Name Is Renée: Ruth Kapp Hartz's Story as a Hidden Child in Nazi-Occupied France.* New York: Oxford University Press, 1999.

Ingham, Richard. *France.* Austin, TX: Raintree/Steck-Vaughn, 2000.

Maguire, Gregory. *The Good Liar.* New York: Clarion Books, 1999.

Manley, Claudia B. *Secret Agents: Life as a Professional Spy.* New York: Rosen Publishing Group, 2001.

Nardo, Don. *France* (Enchantment of the World). Danbury, CT: Children's Press, 2000.

Platt, Richard. *Spies!* (Eyewitness Books). New York: Dorling Kindersley, 2000.

Spangenburg, Ray, and Kit Moser. *Artificial Satellites.* New York: Franklin Watts, 2001.

Bibliography

Cornick, Martyn, and Peter Morris, compilers. *The French Secret Services: A Selected Bibliography*. New Brunswick, NJ: Transaction Publishers, 1993.

Deacon, Richard. *The French Secret Service*. London: Grafton, 1990.

de Marenches, Alexandre, comte, and David A. Andelman. *The Fourth World War: Diplomacy and Espionage in the Age of Terrorism*. New York: William Morrow, 1992.

Devries, Henry P., Nina M. Galston, Regina Loening, and George Berman. *French Law, Constitution and Selective Legislation*. Huntington, NY: Juris Publishing, 1988.

Faligot, Roger, and Pascal Krop (translator) and W.D. Halls. *La Piscine: The French Secret Services Since 1944*. Oxford & New York: Basil Blackwell, 1989.

The French Secret Services. Vol. 6 in the International Organizations Series. Oxford, England: Clio Press, 1993.

Lewis, Peter. "French DGSE Adapts to New World Order." *Jane's Intelligence Review*, July 2000, pp. 12–13

Oxford American Children's Encyclopedia. New York: Robert Bentley, 1998.

Pennetier, Jean-Marc. "Review Article: The Springtime of French Intelligence." *Intelligence and National Security 11*, No. 4, October 1996, pp. 780–798.

Porch, Douglas. "French Intelligence Culture: A Historical and Political Perspective." *Intelligence and National Security 10*, No. 3, July 1995, pp. 486–511.

Porch, Douglas. *The French Secret Services: From the Dreyfus Affair to the Gulf War.* New York: Farrar, Straus & Giroux, 1995.

Rieul, Roland. *Escape into Espionage: The True Story of a French Patriot in World War II.* New York: Walker and Company, 1987.

Richelson, Jeffrey T. *Foreign Intelligence Organizations.* Cambridge, MA: Ballinger, 1988.

Sunday Times Insight Team Staff. *Rainbow Warrior: The French Attempt to Sink Greenpeace.* London, England: Hutchinson, 1986

West, Nigel. *Games of Intelligence: The Classified Conflict of International Espionage Revealed.* London, England: Crown, 1989.

World Book Encyclopedia. Chicago: World Book, Inc., 2000.

Index

Credits

About the Author

Patti Polisar is a writer living in Cambridge, Massachusetts. Her curiosity about France dates from a country report she presented to her sixth-grade class. She was wearing Chanel lipstick and a beret.

Photo Credits

Cover © AFP Photo/Michel Clement; pp. 5, 42 © AP/Wide World Photos; pp. 7, 11, 12, 25, 26, 30, 32, 33, 36 © Hulton/Archive/Getty Images, Inc.; p. 10 © Bettmann/Corbis; pp. 13, 14, 38 © Corbis; p. 18 © 2002 Geoatlas; p. 19 © Astrium Space; p. 40 © Yves Debay/Corbis; p. 44 © Matthias Kulka/Corbis; pp. 46, 52 © AFP/Corbis; p. 50 © Reuters Newmedia, Inc./Corbis.

Editor

Jill Jarnow

Design and Layout

Thomas Forget